CHINESE LEGENDS FOR KIDS

FOR KIDS

EMPERORS, DRAGONS, GODS, HEROES,
MYTHS & MORE FROM ANCIENT CHINA

FREE BONUS FROM HBA:
EBOOK BUNDLE

TABLE OF CONTENTS

INTRODUCTION: WELCOME TO THE WORLD OF CHINESE LEGENDS!

Imagine a world where dragons soar through the skies, mischievous monkeys leap from treetop to treetop, and brave heroes save entire kingdoms! Legends are magical stories that have been passed down from generation to generation. These stories are not only fun to hear but also teach us valuable lessons about life, friendship, courage, and kindness. A legend might tell the tale of a clever trickster, a powerful emperor, or a magical goddess living on the moon. But no matter what the story is about, it always holds a hidden lesson for us to discover.

Chinese legends are some of the oldest stories in the world. Many of them began thousands of years ago, long before the modern cities of today existed. Back then, people told stories to explain how the world worked—like how the sun rises, why the seasons change, or what happens when we are kind to others. These tales also helped people learn what it means to be brave, wise, or kind. By reading these stories, you'll explore a world full of magic, courage, and imagination.

A Peek into China's Ancient History and Traditions

China has a rich and ancient history. Long ago, China was ruled by mighty emperors who built great palaces and walls to protect their people. It was a place where scholars studied the stars, farmers grew rice by the river, and merchants traveled along the Silk Road, bringing treasures from distant lands. Throughout all these years, stories were told to make sense of the world around them.

In ancient times, people believed that dragons brought rain to help crops grow, and the moon held a beautiful goddess named Chang'e. Heroes like Mulan fought for their families and kingdoms, while gods like the Jade Emperor ruled from the heavens. Even animals, like the carp that transformed into a dragon, found their place in these stories, teaching important lessons about perseverance and bravery.

These legends connect with Chinese traditions in so many ways. Festivals, like the Mid-Autumn Festival, celebrate the tale of Chang'e, and the Chinese New Year brings the story of Nian, the monster who feared fireworks and red decorations. Through these stories, children and adults alike understand the meaning behind many customs, foods, and celebrations that are still enjoyed today. By reading these legends, you'll see how China's past is woven into its present.

How These Tales Shape Chinese Culture Today

Even today, the wisdom found in Chinese legends is all around us. You might spot statues of the Laughing Buddha in homes and temples, bringing joy and good fortune. During the Lunar New Year, families celebrate with bright red lanterns and lion dances to keep away bad luck, just like the villagers did in the story of Nian.

These stories are not just about entertainment—they show us how to live. The tale of the Monkey King teaches us to never give up, even when the journey is tough. The story of Mulan reminds us that anyone, no matter who they are, can be a hero. Legends like these help people, young and old, understand values such as kindness, bravery, and respect for others. They also encourage us to dream big and believe that anything is possible.

What's wonderful about these legends is that they continue to inspire new stories. You'll see traces of these old tales in books, movies, and TV shows today. Maybe you've heard of Kung Fu Panda or seen the live-action Mulan movie—these are modern retellings inspired by ancient Chinese stories. Legends live on because they spark imagination and teach lessons that never grow old.

This book is your gateway to a world full of adventure! As you turn each page, you'll meet dragons that bring rain, gods who rule the heavens, and tricksters who love to stir up trouble. You'll read about heroes like Mulan and the Monkey King, who show us how to be courageous and clever. You'll explore the story of the Jade Emperor and discover how the animals of the Chinese zodiac earned their place in the calendar.

As you read each chapter, think about the lessons hidden in these stories. What can you learn from the Monkey King's mischievous ways? How does the tale of the carp becoming a dragon inspire you to keep trying, even when things seem hard? These legends are not only fun to read but also full of ideas that you can use in your own life.

You'll also discover some of the traditions and festivals that keep these legends alive today. Maybe you'll want to celebrate the Mid-Autumn Festival with mooncakes or try creating your own dragon mask for Chinese New Year. Each story opens a door to understanding more about Chinese culture and the values that have been passed down for generations.

So, get ready to dive into a world of wonder! With each story, you'll travel to magical places, meet unforgettable characters, and discover valuable lessons along the way. Whether you want to laugh with the Monkey King, dream with Chang'e on the moon, or battle alongside Mulan, this book has something for everyone.

Let your imagination take flight like a dragon in the clouds! The adventure starts now—are you ready to begin?

CHAPTER 1: THE LEGEND OF THE DRAGON KING - GUARDIAN OF THE SEAS

＊◇◇◉◇◇＊

Deep beneath the waves of the ocean, in a palace made of shimmering pearls and coral, lives the Dragon King—one of the most powerful and respected figures in Chinese mythology. The Dragon King is not just one dragon but a title passed among several rulers of the seas, with each Dragon King governing a different ocean. Together, these mighty dragons are protectors of the water, rain, and all creatures that swim below. They have long, serpent-like bodies, shining scales, and long whiskers that flow gracefully with the currents.

In Chinese legends, dragons are not fire-breathing monsters like those found in other myths. Instead, they are wise and powerful beings associated with water and life. The Dragon King is known to be a fair ruler who ensures the seas remain calm and provides much-needed rain to nourish the crops on land. If treated with respect, the Dragon King offers blessings. But if angered, his rage could stir up storms and massive waves! This makes the Dragon King both admired and feared.

Tales of the Dragon King's Adventures Beneath the Waves

The Dragon King's palace is hidden at the bottom of the sea, surrounded by fish, sea turtles, and glowing jellyfish. Here, he rules over his watery kingdom and listens to the needs of sea creatures and fishermen. Many stories tell of his adventures and the times he came to help both the people on land and the creatures of the sea.

One of the most famous stories tells how the Dragon King helped a young boy named Liu. During a terrible drought, the rivers dried up, and the crops withered under the blazing sun. The villagers prayed for rain, but none came. So Liu decided to venture to the Dragon King's palace beneath the ocean to ask for help. Brave and determined, Liu swam deep into the sea, dodging schools of fish and swirling currents, until he found the Dragon King's palace.

When Liu asked the Dragon King to bring rain, the mighty dragon listened carefully. Touched by the boy's bravery and concern for his village, the Dragon King agreed to send rain clouds to the land. Soon after, the skies darkened, and rain poured down, saving the crops and filling the rivers once again. Liu returned to his village a hero, and the people celebrated the Dragon King's kindness.

In another story, the Dragon King faced off against a sea monster that was terrorizing ships. The creature had sharp teeth, glowing red eyes, and a terrifying roar that could shake the ocean floor. But the Dragon King, with his majestic power, summoned waves and lightning to battle the monster. After a long struggle, the Dragon King emerged victorious, restoring peace to the sea. This tale teaches us that the Dragon King is not only wise but also courageous, willing to protect those in need.

The Importance of Dragons in Chinese Culture

In Chinese culture, dragons are seen as symbols of power, protection, and good fortune. Unlike the scary dragons of other cultures, Chinese dragons bring blessings and are often called upon during festivals and ceremonies. The Dragon King himself is believed to have control over water, rain, and weather, which are essential for a good harvest. This connection between dragons and nature is why many farmers prayed to the Dragon King to send rain during dry seasons.

Dragons are also celebrated during the Dragon Boat Festival, where people race beautifully decorated boats shaped like dragons across rivers and lakes. This tradition is not only exciting but also honors the spirit of the dragon and brings the community together. In ancient times, emperors considered themselves to be like dragons— powerful rulers who protected their people and kept the land prosperous.

Even today, the image of the dragon appears everywhere in Chinese art, architecture, and clothing. You'll see dragons on temple roofs, festival decorations, and even embroidered on the robes of ancient emperors. The Dragon King's presence is still felt in modern China, where dragons are a beloved symbol of strength, luck, and protection.

Lessons from the Dragon King: Protection, Power, and Respect

The stories of the Dragon King are not just exciting tales—they also carry important lessons. One of the most important lessons is about protection. The Dragon King uses his power to protect both the sea creatures and the people on land, showing us that true strength lies in caring for others. Just like the Dragon King calmed the storms and brought rain to the villagers, we can help those around us by being kind and supportive.

Another lesson we learn from the Dragon King is about responsibility and power. The Dragon King has the power to create storms and calm the seas, but he must use his abilities wisely. This teaches us that having power comes with responsibility. It's not enough to be strong—we must use our strength to do good and make the world a better place.

Finally, the Dragon King's stories remind us about the importance of respect for nature. The sea is vast and powerful, and we must treat it with care, just as the villagers respected the Dragon King by offering prayers and thanks. When we respect nature—

whether it's the ocean, rivers, forests, or animals—
we help keep the world balanced and healthy.

The Dragon King's tales encourage us to be kind,
brave, and respectful. Just like Liu, who bravely
asked the Dragon King for rain, we can all make a
difference when we show courage and care for
others. And like the Dragon King, we can use our
talents and strengths to protect the world around
us.

So, the next time you see a dragon decoration or
watch the rain fall from the sky, think of the Dragon
King swimming beneath the waves, watching over
the seas and rivers, and bringing balance to the
world. His story is a reminder that even the most
powerful beings can choose kindness, courage, and
wisdom—and so can we!

CHAPTER 2: THE STORY OF CHANG'E - THE MOON GODDESS

———✦◇◈◇✦———

High up in the night sky, far above the clouds and stars, lives Chang'e, the Moon Goddess. Her story is one of love, sacrifice, and magic, and it has been told for centuries. On nights when the moon is full and bright, people in China remember her legend. They gather with their families, eat delicious mooncakes, and look up at the moon, wondering if they might catch a glimpse of Chang'e or the Jade Rabbit hopping by her side. Let's dive into this beautiful story and discover how Chang'e became the Moon Goddess and what lessons her tale teaches us!

How Chang'e Flew to the Moon

A long, long time ago, Chang'e was the wife of Hou Yi, a famous archer. Hou Yi was known throughout the land for his incredible skill with a bow and arrow, and he was celebrated as a hero. One day, the Jade Emperor—who ruled both the heavens and the earth—noticed that ten suns had risen in the sky instead of just one. The heat from these suns was scorching the land, drying up rivers, and withering crops. The people were desperate for help.

The Jade Emperor asked Hou Yi to use his skills to save the world. Hou Yi took his mighty bow and shot down nine of the suns, leaving just one in the sky to provide light and warmth. The people were saved, and Hou Yi became a beloved hero. As a reward, the Jade Emperor gave Hou Yi a special gift—a potion of immortality. This magical potion would allow the person who drank it to live forever and ascend to the heavens.

However, Hou Yi did not want to leave Chang'e behind. Instead of drinking the potion, he decided to keep it safe and hidden. But one day, a greedy man tried to steal the potion while Hou Yi was away. To protect it, Chang'e made a bold decision—she drank the potion herself. Suddenly, Chang'e began to float, rising higher and higher into the sky. She flew all the way to the moon, where she would stay forever.

Even though Chang'e became immortal, she missed Hou Yi deeply. Alone on the moon, she gazed down at the earth every night, longing to be with the people she loved. But from that moment on, the moon became her home, and she became known as the Moon Goddess.

The Legend of the Jade Rabbit and Its Friendship with Chang'e

Living alone on the moon could have been a very lonely experience for Chang'e, but she was not completely alone. According to legend, a kind and magical Jade Rabbit lives on the moon with her. The story of the Jade Rabbit begins with three animals—a rabbit, a fox, and a monkey—who were asked by the gods to find food to help a hungry traveler. The fox and monkey brought food they had found, but the rabbit, having nothing to give, offered himself. Touched by the rabbit's selflessness, the gods transformed him into the Jade

Rabbit and gave him a home on the moon, where he became Chang'e's companion.

Together, Chang'e and the Jade Rabbit became close friends. It is said that the Jade Rabbit spends his days mixing potions, grinding herbs, and preparing magical elixirs in a large mortar. Sometimes, people on earth even imagine they can see his shadow when the moon is full—if you look carefully, you might spot the outline of a rabbit!

Chang'e and the Jade Rabbit share stories, watch over the world below, and remind us that even in times of loneliness, friendship and kindness can bring comfort. Their tale teaches us the importance of companionship and how even the smallest acts of kindness, like the rabbit's, can have lasting meaning.

Celebrating the Mid-Autumn Festival in Her Honor

Every year, on the 15th day of the eighth lunar month, people in China and other parts of Asia celebrate the Mid-Autumn Festival to honor Chang'e. This special festival is a time for family reunions, delicious food, and looking at the moon. Families gather under the night sky, eat mooncakes (round pastries filled with sweet or savory fillings), and share stories about the Moon Goddess.

During the Mid-Autumn Festival, children carry colorful lanterns shaped like animals or stars, adding magic to the night. Some families light incense and offer fruits to Chang'e as a way to show their respect. It is a time for people to reflect on the importance of family and togetherness, just as Chang'e wishes to be reunited with her loved ones on earth.

The mooncakes eaten during this festival are more than just tasty treats—they are also symbols of unity and completeness. Just like the round shape of the moon, these cakes remind us that even though Chang'e is far away on the moon, the bond between loved ones remains strong.

Lessons from Chang'e: Love, Sacrifice, and Longing

The story of Chang'e is not just a beautiful tale—it also teaches us valuable lessons about love and sacrifice. Chang'e's choice to drink the potion was an act of bravery and protection. She gave up her life on earth to keep the magic potion safe and ensure that it would not fall into the wrong hands. Through her story, we learn that love sometimes means making difficult sacrifices to protect those we care about.

Chang'e's time on the moon also teaches us about longing and how important it is to cherish the moments we share with the people we love. Even though she became immortal, Chang'e's heart still longed for the company of Hou Yi and the people on earth. Her story reminds us to value our time with family and friends because those moments are precious.

The friendship between Chang'e and the Jade Rabbit offers another important lesson—kindness and companionship can help us through even the loneliest times. The Jade Rabbit's selflessness shows us that acts of kindness, no matter how small, can bring joy and meaning to others.

Finally, Chang'e's story teaches us about hope and renewal. Just as the moon changes from new to full each month, we are reminded that life is always moving in cycles. Even when we experience sadness or separation, there is always the hope of new beginnings, just like the moon reappearing after a dark night.

The story of Chang'e and the Jade Rabbit has captured the imaginations of people for generations. When you look up at the moon, think of Chang'e sitting in her palace with the Jade Rabbit by her side. Their story teaches us that even when we feel far from the ones we love, the light of friendship, love, and kindness will always shine through.

So, the next time you see the full moon glowing in the sky, make a wish for Chang'e and the Jade Rabbit. And who knows? Maybe, just maybe, she'll send a little moonlight your way to remind you that you are never truly alone.

CHAPTER 3: THE TALE OF THE MONKEY KING - JOURNEY TO THE WEST

—————— ✦◇◇◉◇◇✦ ——————

Have you ever imagined what it would be like to meet a mischievous monkey with magical powers? In Chinese legends, the Monkey King—also known as Sun Wukong—is one of the most exciting and beloved characters of all time. He is clever, funny, and full of energy, but he also learns important lessons about bravery, wisdom, and growth during his adventures. So, let's swing through the trees and dive into the incredible world of the Monkey King!

Who Is the Mischievous Monkey King?

The Monkey King's story begins on a magical mountain where a special stone gave birth to a monkey. This was no ordinary monkey—he was destined for greatness. He could talk, walk upright, and jump higher than any other creature in the forest. The monkeys of the mountain quickly made him their king because he was so smart and fearless.

But being king of the monkeys wasn't enough for Sun Wukong. He wanted to become even more powerful. He traveled far and wide, learning magical skills from wise masters and becoming stronger with each new adventure. The Monkey King could transform into different animals, summon clouds to ride through the sky, and even make himself invisible!

With all these abilities, Sun Wukong became quite confident—maybe a little too confident! His playful tricks soon became trouble, as he began to challenge the gods and cause mischief in the heavens. But every legend needs a twist, and the Monkey King's story is all about how he learns to use his powers for good.

His Magical Staff and Incredible Adventures

One of the most famous parts of the Monkey King's story is his magical staff, called the Ruyi Jingu Bang. This wasn't just any ordinary staff—it could shrink to the size of a needle or grow as tall as a mountain! The staff became Sun Wukong's favorite weapon, and with it, he fought off powerful enemies, including demons and monsters.

But the adventures didn't stop there. Sun Wukong became famous for his strength and cleverness. One of his most exciting adventures is told in the legend of Journey to the West. In this story, the Monkey King joins a monk named Xuanzang on a long journey to find sacred Buddhist scriptures. Along the way, Sun Wukong faces many challenges, from fighting fierce demons to solving tricky puzzles.

On this journey, the Monkey King teams up with two companions: Pigsy, a greedy pig spirit, and Sandy, a river demon. The three of them help Xuanzang on his mission, protecting him from danger and learning important lessons about friendship, patience, and teamwork. While Sun Wukong's mischievous side causes trouble now and then, his clever tricks often save the day.

How the Monkey King Learned to Be Wise and Brave

Even though the Monkey King started out as a mischievous troublemaker, his adventures taught him some valuable lessons. During his journey with Xuanzang, Sun Wukong learned that being strong isn't just about having magical powers—it's also about using those powers wisely.

One of the hardest lessons for the Monkey King was learning to control his temper. In the beginning, he would rush into fights without thinking, using his strength to defeat anyone in his way. But as he traveled with Xuanzang, he realized that bravery also meant knowing when to be patient and finding peaceful solutions.

By the end of his journey, Sun Wukong had grown from a mischievous monkey into a wise hero. He earned the respect of the gods and found peace within himself. Through his adventures, the Monkey King discovered that true strength comes not just from power, but from wisdom, kindness, and understanding.

Lessons from the Monkey King: Strength, Cleverness, and Growth

The tale of the Monkey King is more than just an exciting adventure—it's also filled with important lessons that we can all learn from.

First, the Monkey King teaches us about the power of cleverness. Even though Sun Wukong was smaller than many of his enemies, he often outsmarted them with his quick thinking. His story reminds us that brains can be just as important as brawn, especially when we face challenges.

Second, the Monkey King's journey shows us the importance of growth and learning from our mistakes. Sun Wukong wasn't perfect—he made a lot of mistakes along the way. But each time he faced a challenge, he became wiser and stronger. His story encourages us to keep learning, even when things get tough.

Finally, the Monkey King's tale is a reminder that strength isn't just about fighting—it's also about kindness and self-control. Sun Wukong started his adventures thinking that power meant winning battles, but he learned that true strength comes from using his abilities to help others.

Sun Wukong's adventures have been told and retold for centuries, and his story remains one of the most popular in Chinese culture. Kids and adults alike admire the Monkey King's daring spirit, quick wit, and big heart. His journey from a mischievous troublemaker to a wise hero shows us that anyone can grow, change, and become better with time.

So, the next time you feel like mischief is calling, think of the Monkey King. Use your cleverness, but don't forget to be kind and wise too! And who knows? Maybe you'll go on your own adventure one day—just like Sun Wukong on his journey to the West.

CHAPTER 4: THE WEAVER AND THE COWHERD - A LOVE ACROSS THE STARS

Long ago, in the vast sky, there lived a beautiful young girl named Zhinu, the Weaver Girl. She was no ordinary girl—Zhinu was a goddess who could weave the most beautiful clouds in the heavens, creating colors and patterns that sparkled like rainbows. Her job was to weave the sky with these magical clouds, filling it with light and wonder. But despite all the beauty she created, Zhinu felt lonely. She spent her days weaving and dreaming of something more—she longed for love and adventure beyond the heavens.

Down on Earth, there lived a kind-hearted young man named Niulang, the Cowherd. Niulang was a humble farmer who took care of a small herd of cows. Though his life was simple, he was happy, surrounded by nature and his animals. But, like Zhinu, he too dreamed of love—of someone to share his life with.

And so, the stars aligned, and fate brought the two together.

How the Weaver Girl and the Cowherd Fell in Love

One day, Zhinu's curiosity got the best of her. She decided to leave the heavens and visit the Earth disguised as a mortal girl. As she wandered through a beautiful forest, she met Niulang by chance. From the moment they saw each other, it was as if the stars themselves had connected their hearts. Zhinu and Niulang fell deeply in love, and they decided to stay together, creating a happy life on Earth.

Niulang's cows loved Zhinu just as much as he did. With her by his side, life seemed perfect. The Weaver Girl and the Cowherd spent their days laughing, farming, and sharing stories under the bright sky. They were inseparable, and together they built a life full of joy and love.

But love between a goddess and a mortal was not something the gods would easily allow. When the mighty Queen Mother of the West, Zhinu's mother, found out that her daughter had fallen in love with a human, she became very angry. She believed that gods and mortals could not live together, so she ordered Zhinu to return to the heavens, separating her from Niulang forever.

Heartbroken, Niulang refused to give up. With the help of a magical cow from his herd, Niulang flew to the heavens, determined to be reunited with his beloved Zhinu. But just as they were about to embrace, the Queen Mother of the West drew a river of stars across the sky, creating the Milky Way to keep them apart.

The Bridge of Magpies and the Qixi Festival

Even though Zhinu and Niulang were separated by the Milky Way, their love was so strong that it touched the hearts of the animals and birds. Every year, on the seventh day of the seventh lunar month, magpies from all over the world would gather to help the two lovers meet again. They would form a bridge across the Milky Way, allowing

Zhinu and Niulang to cross the river of stars and be together for just one night.

This magical night became known as Qixi, the Chinese Valentine's Day. To this day, people celebrate the Qixi Festival by looking up at the night sky, hoping to catch a glimpse of the stars where the Weaver Girl and the Cowherd meet. Children make wishes, and couples exchange gifts, just like Zhinu and Niulang shared their love across the stars.

The stars Altair and Vega—which represent Niulang and Zhinu—shine brightly in the night sky, separated by the Milky Way but forever connected in spirit. On the night of Qixi, it's said that if the sky is clear and the stars are bright, the magpies have built their bridge once again, reuniting the lovers for their special night.

Lessons from the Weaver and the Cowherd: Patience, Love, and Hope

The story of the Weaver Girl and the Cowherd teaches us that true love is patient and never gives up, even when faced with challenges. Zhinu and Niulang's love was so powerful that even a river of stars could not keep them apart forever. Their story reminds us that love is worth waiting for, and that sometimes, patience is the greatest strength of all.

The tale also shows us the importance of hope. Even though Zhinu and Niulang could only meet once a year, they never lost hope. They believed in their love, and the animals around them believed in it too. Just like the magpies who built a bridge across the Milky Way, we can always find a way to bring people together if we have hope in our hearts.

Finally, this story reminds us to treasure the moments we share with the people we love. Even though the Weaver Girl and the Cowherd could only be together for one night each year, they cherished every second. Whether we have a lot of time or just a little, it's important to make the most of it and show kindness and love to those around us.

The legend of the Weaver Girl and the Cowherd has been passed down for generations, inspiring people with its message of love, patience, and hope. Their story shines brightly in the night sky, reminding us that no matter how far apart we may be, love can always bring us together.

So, the next time you see the Milky Way stretching across the sky, think of Zhinu and Niulang. Look for the stars of Altair and Vega, and make a wish.

Who knows? Maybe the magpies are building their bridge at that very moment, reuniting the two lovers under the watchful gaze of the night sky.

And remember, just like the Weaver Girl and the Cowherd, we too can create bridges with patience, love, and hope—bridges that connect us to the people we care about, no matter where they are.

CHAPTER 5: THE LEGEND OF THE WHITE SNAKE - A TALE OF LOVE AND TRANSFORMATION

Long ago, in ancient China, there lived a powerful spirit in the form of a white snake. But this was no ordinary snake—she was a magical being who had lived for thousands of years, studying the ways of the universe and growing wise and powerful. One day, she transformed into a beautiful woman named Bai Suzhen, leaving behind her snake form to experience life among humans. What she did not expect was to fall deeply in love with a mortal man, and so begins the legend of the White Snake—a story of love, transformation, and courage.

Who Was the White Snake Spirit?

The White Snake Spirit, known as Bai Suzhen, was a magical being that had lived for centuries. Over the years, she learned many skills, including the arts of healing and medicine, using her powers to help others. Unlike other spirits who may have used their magic selfishly, Bai Suzhen wanted to do good. Her heart was filled with kindness, and she longed to see what it would be like to live among people.

One spring day, as Bai Suzhen wandered the world in her human form, she arrived at West Lake near the city of Hangzhou. It was a place of incredible beauty, with peaceful waters and blossoming flowers. There, she met a kind and gentle man named Xu Xian, a scholar who worked as an herbalist. From the moment they met, Bai Suzhen and Xu Xian felt a connection that neither of them could explain. Their love story began that day by the shimmering waters of West Lake.

Her Forbidden Love with a Human

Although Bai Suzhen looked like a human woman, she carried a secret—she was still, in essence, a spirit in the form of a snake, and in ancient times, spirits were not supposed to live among humans or fall in love with them. But Bai Suzhen's heart told her otherwise. She knew her love for Xu Xian was real, and she wanted to spend her life with him.

After meeting. Xu Xian quickly fell in love with Bai Suzhen's beauty and kindness. He admired her ability to heal others and was amazed by how gentle she was with every living thing. It wasn't long before the two decided to get married and live a peaceful life together.

For a time, their love seemed perfect. Bai Suzhen and Xu Xian worked side by side, helping people with their herbs and medicines. Their little home was filled with happiness, and it seemed like nothing could come between them. But there was one person who did not approve of their love—a powerful monk named Fa Hai.

How the White Snake Overcame Challenges for Love

Fa Hai, the monk, believed that spirits like Bai Suzhen did not belong in the human world. He was convinced that Bai Suzhen's presence would bring harm to Xu Xian and everyone around them. Determined to break the couple apart, Fa Hai tricked Xu Xian into giving his wife a special wine during the Dragon Boat Festival.

The wine, known for its mystical properties, forced Bai Suzhen to transform back into her white snake form in front of Xu Xian. Xu Xian was terrified. He couldn't believe that his beloved wife was, in fact, a magical snake spirit. Overwhelmed with fear, Xu Xian collapsed and fell into a deep sleep.

Heartbroken but determined to save her husband, Bai Suzhen embarked on a dangerous journey to find a cure. She traveled far and wide until she reached the sacred Kunlun Mountains, where she found a magical herb capable of reviving Xu Xian. Using all her courage and love, she brought the herb back and saved his life.

However, their troubles were far from over. Fa Hai captured Xu Xian and took him to a temple, locking him away so that Bai Suzhen could never see him again. Despite the obstacles, Bai Suzhen refused to give up. With the help of her loyal friend, the Green Snake Spirit, she stormed the temple, using her magic and bravery to free her husband from Fa Hai's clutches. Even though she faced great danger, Bai Suzhen fought not out of anger, but out of love and determination.

Lessons from the White Snake: Compassion, Change, and Bravery

The story of the White Snake teaches us many important lessons. Bai Suzhen's love for Xu Xian showed that true love can overcome even the greatest challenges. She never gave up on her husband, even when things seemed impossible. Her story reminds us that love is not always easy, but it is worth fighting for.

Bai Suzhen also teaches us about compassion. Even though she had great power, she used it to help others. Instead of being selfish with her abilities, she chose to heal and protect the people around her. This part of the legend reminds us that kindness is one of the greatest strengths anyone can have.

The legend also shows the importance of change and growth. Bai Suzhen transformed from a spirit into a human, learning new things along the way. Just like Bai Suzhen, we too can change and grow, learning from our experiences and becoming better people. The story encourages us to embrace new challenges and believe in the power of transformation.

Finally, Bai Suzhen's story is one of bravery. She faced great dangers to protect the person she loved, showing that bravery isn't just about strength—it's about standing up for what matters most. The White Snake's journey teaches us that courage comes in many forms, whether it's fighting for someone we love or simply being kind in a difficult world.

A Love That Stands the Test of Time

The legend of the White Snake is one of China's most beloved stories, passed down through generations as a tale of love, sacrifice, and transformation. Even today, it continues to inspire books, operas, and movies, reminding people of the power of love and the importance of compassion.

So, the next time you see a beautiful lake or a white snake gliding through the grass, think of Bai Suzhen and her story. Remember the lessons of patience, kindness, and bravery, and know that love—just like Bai Suzhen's—can overcome even the greatest challenges. And who knows? Maybe, like Bai Suzhen, you too will find that with compassion and courage, anything is possible.

CHAPTER 6: THE STORY OF NIAN
- THE MONSTER OF THE NEW YEAR

A long, long time ago, in a small village in ancient China, the people lived in fear of a terrifying monster called Nian. This was no ordinary creature—Nian was enormous, with sharp claws, glowing eyes, and a mouth large enough to swallow anything in its path. Each year, during the coldest winter night, Nian would awaken from his sleep in the mountains and come down to the village, destroying crops, homes, and scaring the people away. For many years, the villagers had no idea how to stop him. But one day, they discovered a way to defeat the fearsome monster using courage, cleverness, and celebration.

How the Villagers Defeated Nian with Fireworks and Drums

Every year, when Nian came down from the mountains, the people would flee in fear, leaving their homes behind. They hid in the forest, hoping that Nian wouldn't find them. But one year, a wise old man came to the village. He told the people that they didn't have to live in fear of Nian anymore.

"I've heard stories about Nian," the old man said. "This monster is afraid of loud noises, the color red, and bright lights." The villagers were surprised. How could a powerful creature like Nian be afraid of such simple things? But they trusted the old man and decided to try his plan.

The villagers began decorating their homes with red paper and ribbons. They hung bright red lanterns outside their doors and wore red clothing to scare Nian away. They also gathered all the drums and cymbals they could find. On the night of Nian's expected arrival, the villagers stayed in the village instead of running away.

When Nian appeared, roaring and stomping through the streets, the villagers beat their drums and banged their cymbals as loud as they could. Firecrackers exploded in bursts of light, and lanterns glowed brightly in the night. The sudden noise, lights, and flashes of red terrified Nian, and the monster ran back to the mountains, never to return. From that day on, the villagers celebrated their victory over Nian with a great celebration, which became known as Chinese New Year!

Celebrating Chinese New Year with Traditions and Customs

The story of Nian is why Chinese New Year, also called the Spring Festival, is celebrated with fireworks, red decorations, and loud music. Families come together to welcome the new year and drive away any bad luck—just like the villagers once scared off the monster Nian.

On New Year's Eve, families gather for a big feast with delicious foods. Dumplings, fish, noodles, and sweets are all part of the celebration, with each dish carrying its own special meaning. For example, long noodles symbolize long life, while fish represents prosperity.

People also give out red envelopes called "hongbao" with money inside. These envelopes are given to children as a way of wishing them good fortune for the year ahead. Another important tradition is cleaning the house before the new year begins. This symbolizes sweeping away the old and making room for good luck and new beginnings.

The most exciting part of the celebration is the fireworks and lion dances! The sound of firecrackers, drums, and cymbals fills the air as performers dress up as lions to dance through the streets, bringing joy and chasing away bad spirits—just like the villagers did to defeat Nian.

Chinese New Year is not just about loud noises and fun decorations; it's also about family, friendship, and new beginnings. It's a time to reflect on the past year and look forward to the future with hope and joy.

Lessons from Nian: Courage, Celebration, and Community

The story of Nian teaches us that even the scariest challenges can be overcome with courage and cleverness. At first, the villagers ran away from Nian, afraid of what he might do. But when they worked together, they found a way to face their fears. This part of the story reminds us that we don't have to face difficult times alone—with the help of others, we can overcome anything.

The story also teaches us about the importance of celebration. The villagers' joy and excitement didn't just defeat Nian—they also brought the community together. Celebrating with family and friends is a way to remind ourselves of the good things in life and share those moments with the people we love.

Another important lesson from the story of Nian is that traditions help keep us connected. The villagers' clever use of red decorations, loud music, and bright lights became the foundation of Chinese New Year traditions. Even today, people follow these customs to welcome good fortune and happiness into their lives.

The story of Nian encourages us to be brave in the face of challenges, celebrate life's victories, and cherish our communities and traditions. Just like the villagers who defeated Nian, we too can find joy, hope, and strength by working together and embracing new beginnings.

Today, the story of Nian lives on through the joy and excitement of Chinese New Year celebrations. Whether it's through the booming sounds of fireworks, the colorful parades, or the warmth of family gatherings, the spirit of the villagers' victory over Nian continues to inspire people of all ages.

So, the next time you hear fireworks popping or see a bright red lantern glowing in the night, think of the brave villagers who defeated Nian. Remember that courage and community can help us overcome any challenge, and celebrations bring us together to share life's joys. And who knows—maybe one day, you'll create your own tradition to share with others, just like the story of Nian became a tradition for people all over the world!

CHAPTER 7: PANGU AND
THE CREATION OF THE WORLD

Long ago, before the world we know existed, there was only darkness—a swirling, silent chaos with no sky, no land, and no sea. But deep within this chaos, something extraordinary began to form: an egg, filled with all the energy of the universe. Inside the egg slept a giant named Pangu, waiting for the right moment to awaken and begin his great task—the creation of the world.

How Pangu Shaped the Heavens and the Earth

After thousands of years inside the egg, Pangu finally opened his eyes. He looked around and saw the swirling darkness around him. But Pangu knew that this chaos had to be separated to create something new. With a mighty swing of his axe, he cracked the egg in two, dividing it into two parts: the light part floated up to become the sky, while the heavier part sank to form the earth.

Pangu knew that the sky and the earth needed to be kept apart, so he stood between them, holding the heavens high above his head. Every day, Pangu grew a little bit taller, pushing the sky higher and higher to make sure it would never fall back down onto the earth. For 18,000 years, Pangu stood like this, separating the heavens from the earth and giving shape to the world we know today.

The Myth of Pangu's Body Becoming Mountains, Rivers, and Trees

Eventually, after many centuries of hard work, Pangu grew tired. His great task was complete—the sky was high, the earth was solid, and the world was ready. So, Pangu gently laid down to rest, knowing that his job was done.

But Pangu's story doesn't end here. In fact, his giant body became the world around us! The legends tell us that when Pangu passed away, his breath became the wind and clouds, and his voice became the thunder that rolls across the skies. His mighty arms and legs transformed into the mountains that rise from the earth, and his blood flowed into rivers that bring life to the land.

Even Pangu's hair and beard found a place in the world—they grew into lush forests and fields. His bones became the precious stones and minerals hidden deep beneath the earth, and his sweat became the morning dew that glistens on leaves and flowers.

And so, every part of Pangu's being became a part of the world, connecting nature to his spirit and leaving behind a beautiful creation filled with life.

Lessons from Pangu: Creation, Endurance, and the Beauty of Nature

The story of Pangu teaches us many important lessons about life, work, and the natural world around us. First, it shows us the power of creation—how everything in the universe has a place and purpose. Pangu's work reminds us that with effort, dedication, and care, we too can shape the world around us and bring good things to life.

This legend also teaches us about endurance. Pangu stood between the heavens and the earth for thousands of years, knowing that his task was too important to give up. Even though it was hard work, Pangu stayed strong until his mission was complete. His story shows us the importance of patience and persistence, especially when we are working on something big or important. Just like Pangu, we can achieve great things when we keep going, even when things are difficult.

Finally, Pangu's story helps us see the beauty of nature. His body becoming mountains, rivers, and trees reminds us that everything in nature is connected. The wind, the rain, the forests, and the animals all work together in harmony. This legend encourages us to respect the natural world and take care of the environment, just as Pangu gave his life to create it.

Pangu's story may be ancient, but it continues to inspire people of all ages. It teaches us that hard work and determination can create something beautiful and that everything around us— mountains, rivers, trees—has its own magic and importance. Whether we are planting a tree, helping a friend, or working on a project, Pangu's legend reminds us to put our hearts into everything we do.

So, the next time you look up at the sky or feel the wind on your face, think of Pangu, the giant who shaped the world with his strength and love. His spirit lives on in the beauty of nature, encouraging us to be kind to the earth and create something wonderful with our own hands. And who knows? Maybe one day, you'll create your own legend, just like Pangu did, leaving a mark on the world for generations to come.

CHAPTER 8: THE JADE EMPEROR - RULER OF HEAVEN

Long, long ago, before there were rulers in the heavens, the earth and the skies were filled with chaos. There were gods, but none of them was powerful enough to bring order. The Jade Emperor wasn't always the most important god. In fact, he was once a kind and wise spirit living a humble life on earth, helping people and creatures wherever he went.

The Jade Emperor's journey to becoming the ruler of all the heavens started with his deep sense of fairness and his love for harmony. After many lifetimes of spreading kindness and wisdom on earth, he earned the respect of the gods. When the time came to choose a ruler for the heavens, the gods all agreed that this gentle but just being should become the Jade Emperor—the Supreme God who would bring peace to the universe.

The Jade Emperor ruled with patience and wisdom, ensuring that every god and spirit knew their duties. But he wasn't just a distant ruler; the Jade Emperor also kept a watchful eye over the people on earth, making sure there was balance between heaven and earth. To keep things in order, he sometimes needed to solve tricky problems, like choosing the animals of the Chinese zodiac—a task that required both fairness and creativity.

The Story of the Great Race and the Chinese Zodiac

The Jade Emperor wanted to create a way for people to measure time and seasons, so he decided to name a year after twelve different animals. But how would he choose which animals to include? He came up with a fun and exciting solution: a great race! The first twelve animals to cross a mighty river would each get a place in the zodiac, with the order of their arrival determining their position.

The animals lined up at the riverbank, eager to start the race. Among them were the rat, ox, tiger, rabbit, dragon, snake, horse, goat, monkey, rooster, dog, and pig. The Jade Emperor watched as the animals prepared to leap into the water and begin the exciting challenge.

As the race began, the ox quickly took the lead, swimming steadily across the river. But unknown to the ox, the clever rat had secretly climbed onto his back! Just before the ox reached the other side, the rat jumped off and scurried to the finish line, becoming the first animal in the zodiac. The ox came in second, followed by the powerful tiger and the quick rabbit, who had hopped from stone to stone to avoid the rushing water.

One of the crowd favorites was the dragon, who came fifth—not because he was slow, but because he had stopped along the way to help villagers by bringing rain to their fields. The rest of the animals arrived in their own time, each with a story about how they overcame challenges during the race. The cheerful pig was the last to arrive, but the Jade Emperor welcomed him with a smile, saying, "Even the slowest has a place."

And so, the twelve animals of the Chinese zodiac were chosen, with each animal symbolizing a different year. The race wasn't just about speed—it was a test of cunning, bravery, teamwork, and perseverance.

Lessons from the Jade Emperor: Leadership, Fairness, and Harmony

The Jade Emperor teaches us many valuable lessons about how to lead with wisdom and kindness. As the Supreme God, he didn't use his power to control others. Instead, he worked to create harmony between the gods, nature, and people on earth. He shows us that being a leader isn't about being the loudest or strongest—it's about making fair decisions that help everyone.

The story of the Great Race teaches us the importance of fairness. The Jade Emperor gave each animal an equal chance, no matter how big or small they were. Even the slow and lazy pig found his way into the zodiac, proving that everyone has value, no matter how long it takes them to reach their goal.

Another lesson from the Jade Emperor is about the importance of teamwork and helping others. The dragon could have easily flown to the finish line first, but he chose to help the villagers in need. This teaches us that sometimes, the right thing to do isn't about winning—it's about making a difference.

The Great Race also reminds us that everyone has their own strengths. The rat's cleverness, the ox's strength, and the rabbit's quick thinking all helped them cross the river in different ways. In life, just like in the race, we all have unique qualities that can help us overcome challenges.

The Jade Emperor's leadership continues to inspire people today, especially during the Lunar New Year celebrations. The Chinese zodiac is not just about marking time—it's also a way to celebrate each person's strengths and the qualities that make us who we are. Each animal in the zodiac teaches us something about ourselves and others, helping us understand the importance of patience, kindness, and hard work.

The Jade Emperor's story also reminds us that life is a journey. Whether we reach our goals quickly, like the rat, or take our time, like the pig, what matters most is that we keep moving forward and help others along the way.

So, the next time you hear a New Year's celebration filled with fireworks and joy, think of the Jade Emperor and his wise leadership. Just like the animals in the zodiac, you have your own special qualities that make you unique. Whether you're brave like the tiger, patient like the ox, or clever like the rat, there's always a place for you in the story of life.

And who knows—maybe one day, you'll find yourself leading with wisdom, just like the Jade Emperor did, bringing harmony and happiness to everyone around you.

CHAPTER 9: THE LEGEND OF MULAN - A BRAVE DAUGHTER'S JOURNEY

Long ago in ancient China, the land faced a great threat. The Emperor sent out a decree calling on all men to join the army and protect their homeland. Every family had to send one man to fight. When the message reached the home of a young girl named Mulan, she knew her family was in trouble. Mulan's father, though brave, was old and weak. He had fought in battles before, and now he was too frail to do so again. But since he had no sons, there was no choice—he would have to go to war.

Mulan couldn't stand the thought of her father suffering on the battlefield. She loved her father dearly and knew he wouldn't survive another war. So, with a brave heart, Mulan made a daring decision—she would go in his place! She put on her father's armor, tied her hair back, and took his sword. Disguising herself as a young man, she quietly left her home under the cover of night, ready to face whatever challenges lay ahead.

Mulan knew the risk she was taking. If anyone discovered that she was a girl, she would be in serious trouble. But Mulan's love for her family gave her the courage to press on. She was determined to do everything she could to protect her father and honor her family.

Her Adventures and Battles in Disguise

When Mulan joined the army, no one suspected her secret. She trained hard alongside the other soldiers, running drills, practicing sword fighting, and preparing for battle. At first, it was tough—Mulan wasn't used to the harsh conditions of army life. But she didn't give up. She worked harder than anyone else, determined to prove herself, and little by little, she gained the respect of her fellow soldiers.

Soon, Mulan found herself marching into battle. Her heart pounded with fear, but she reminded herself why she was there—for her father, her family, and her country. In every fight, Mulan showed bravery and skill, leading her comrades to victory. Her quick thinking saved lives, and she fought fiercely against the enemies threatening her homeland.

One of Mulan's most famous moments came when her army was ambushed by enemies in a narrow mountain pass. Trapped and outnumbered, things looked hopeless. But Mulan came up with a clever plan. Using fireworks and signal flares, she caused an avalanche that swept the enemy soldiers away, giving her army a chance to escape. Thanks to her courage and smart thinking, they won the day!

As time went on, Mulan's reputation as a brave and capable warrior spread throughout the army. She became a trusted leader, helping guide her comrades through many difficult battles. But all this time, no one knew her true identity. Mulan kept her secret close to her heart, knowing that it could cost her everything if it were revealed.

Lessons from Mulan: Courage, Family, and Honor

After years of service, the war finally came to an end. Mulan and her comrades returned home as heroes. The Emperor, hearing of Mulan's bravery, called her to the palace to offer her a great reward. But instead of riches or titles, Mulan asked for only one thing—to return home to her family.

It was then, surrounded by her comrades, that Mulan revealed her true identity. To everyone's amazement, the fierce warrior who had fought alongside them was not a man, but a young woman. The soldiers and the Emperor were stunned, but instead of punishment, they honored Mulan for her bravery and selflessness. She had risked everything, not for fame or fortune, but for love and loyalty to her family.

Mulan's story teaches us many valuable lessons.

Courage is not about being fearless—it's about doing the right thing even when you're scared. Mulan knew the dangers she faced, but she was brave enough to stand up for what she believed in and protect the people she loved.

Family plays a central role in Mulan's story. She chose to fight in place of her father, showing us that family comes first and that love for those we care about can give us strength.

Lastly, honor is an important lesson from Mulan's story. Even though she had to break the rules by disguising herself as a man, Mulan's actions were driven by a deep sense of responsibility. She honored her family, her comrades, and her country by fighting with bravery and loyalty.

A Hero for All Time

Mulan's story has inspired people for centuries. She is a symbol of strength, courage, and love—qualities that remind us all that anyone, no matter their size or appearance, can become a hero. Mulan teaches us that being true to yourself and following your heart can lead to incredible things. Whether you're facing a tough challenge at school or helping a friend in need, you can channel Mulan's bravery and do what's right, even when it's hard.

And just like Mulan, you don't need armor or a sword to be a hero. All it takes is kindness, courage, and a willingness to help others. So, the next time you feel nervous or unsure, think of Mulan and her journey from a quiet village to the battlefield. You have the same bravery inside you—all you need to do is believe in yourself.

Mulan's tale will always remind us that greatness comes from the heart, not from appearances. And as long as we carry her story with us, we'll always remember that we, too, can be heroes in our own unique way.

CHAPTER 10: THE LAUGHING BUDDHA - A SYMBOL OF HAPPINESS

The Laughing Buddha, known as Budai in Chinese, is one of the most beloved figures in Chinese culture. He is not the same Buddha who founded Buddhism, but a joyful monk who became a symbol of happiness, kindness, and good fortune. You've probably seen statues of him before—he has a round belly, a wide grin, and carries a big cloth bag.

So why is the Laughing Buddha always smiling? Well, it's said that Budai found joy in simple things like making people laugh, sharing stories, and helping those in need. His smile reminds us that happiness comes from within and that kindness can bring light to others' lives. Wherever he went, Budai spread joy, laughter, and generosity, making him a beloved figure in both temples and homes.

People believe that rubbing the Laughing Buddha's belly brings good luck! This cheerful monk is also known as the "patron of children and the poor," as he cared deeply for those who had little, always sharing what he had with a happy heart.

Tales of the Laughing Buddha's Travels and Generosity

The Laughing Buddha didn't stay in one place for long—he loved to travel. With nothing more than his big cloth bag and a walking stick, Budai wandered from town to town, meeting new people and spreading joy wherever he went.

One popular story tells of Budai arriving in a small village where people were worried about a bad harvest. The villagers were sad, but Budai sat under a tree, smiling and laughing as if all their problems had already disappeared. Curious, the children of the village gathered around him. Budai told funny stories and gave them small gifts from his bag. Soon, the whole village was filled with laughter, and even the adults began to smile.

Budai didn't have much, but he shared whatever he could—sometimes coins, sometimes toys or food. Whenever he gave something away, his joy seemed to grow even bigger, teaching everyone that true happiness comes from sharing what you have with others.

Another tale says that one day, Budai found a group of people arguing over a small amount of money. He opened his bag and gave away the last of his coins to stop the argument. "Happiness is better than gold," he said with a chuckle, and the people felt ashamed of their greed. They promised to value kindness over wealth, thanks to Budai's wise and cheerful example.

Lessons from the Laughing Buddha: Kindness, Joy, and Sharing

The Laughing Buddha's tales are more than just funny stories—they carry important life lessons for all of us.

First, Budai teaches us the importance of kindness. He didn't wait to be asked for help—he gave freely, whether it was food, a coin, or a smile. His kindness shows us that small acts of generosity can make a big difference in someone's life.

The Laughing Buddha also reminds us that joy is something we can share. No matter where Budai went, he found a reason to smile, even during tough times. His laughter was contagious, helping others see the good in every situation. From Budai, we learn that even when things aren't perfect, a positive attitude can brighten our day and the lives of those around us.

Lastly, Budai's stories teach us about the importance of sharing. He didn't hold on to what he had—he gave it away freely and found happiness in doing so. Budai shows us that sharing isn't just about giving objects—it's also about sharing time, laughter, and kindness with others. Whether it's a kind word or a helping hand, sharing makes the world a better place.

The Laughing Buddha reminds us that happiness isn't found in things—it's found in how we treat others. You don't need a big bag of gifts or gold to spread joy like Budai did. A smile, a kind word, or a simple act of generosity can brighten someone's day.

Think about a time when you made someone smile. How did it make you feel? Just like the Laughing Buddha, you can make the world a little brighter by spreading kindness wherever you go. Whether it's helping a friend, sharing a snack, or telling a funny story, your actions can make a difference.

And remember, the Laughing Buddha teaches us to find joy in simple things—a sunny day, a friendly hello, or the sound of laughter. Even when things are hard, try to find something to be thankful for. Just like Budai's smile brought hope to those around him, your joy can inspire others to find their own happiness.

The Laughing Buddha's story is a reminder that life is better when we share kindness and joy with others. Whether we're facing a challenge or enjoying a happy moment, we can all learn from Budai's example:

Be kind to others and help whenever you can.

Share your happiness and make someone smile.

Find joy in the little things, and spread that joy wherever you go.

The next time you see a statue of the Laughing Buddha, remember his stories and the lessons he teaches. Try rubbing his belly for good luck, and then go out and spread some joy, just like Budai did long ago. And who knows? Your kindness might just make someone's day a little brighter!

CHAPTER 11: THE STORY OF YU THE GREAT - TAMER OF THE FLOODS

A long, long time ago in ancient China, a terrible flood covered the land. The waters rose higher and higher, washing away homes, farms, and villages. Crops couldn't grow, people had to flee from their homes, and no one knew how to stop the endless rain. The flood seemed unstoppable, causing misery for everyone—until a hero named Yu stepped forward.

Yu the Great was not just an ordinary man—he was known for his bravery, wisdom, and unshakable determination. The Emperor asked Yu to find a way to stop the flood and save the land. It was a difficult task, but Yu accepted the challenge, knowing that the fate of China depended on it. Instead of trying to block the water, which had failed many times before, Yu came up with a clever plan.

Yu believed the best way to fight the flood was to work with the water, not against it. He noticed how rivers naturally flowed towards the sea and decided to guide the floodwaters safely instead of stopping them. For thirteen long years, Yu traveled across China, digging canals, building dams, and shaping rivers so the water could flow freely without causing harm. He worked tirelessly, sometimes using just a simple shovel and his own hands to carve out new paths for the water.

His Wisdom in Building Canals and Dams

Yu's most important lesson was that understanding nature's rhythms was the key to success. Instead of trying to block the flood all at once, he guided the water into different paths, letting it flow safely back to rivers and the sea. Every canal Yu built allowed the water to spread out evenly, and dams helped hold back the strongest currents.

Yu didn't just work alone—he inspired people across the land to help. Villagers and farmers worked side by side with Yu, digging canals and building dams that would protect their homes and crops. They trusted Yu because he never gave up, even when the work seemed impossible. Yu's leadership showed everyone that when people work together, even the greatest challenges can be overcome.

It wasn't easy, though. Yu traveled through rugged mountains, dense forests, and dangerous rivers.

Sometimes he slept on the ground under the stars, too focused on his task to return home. In fact, Yu was so dedicated to his work that he didn't return to his family for many years, knowing that the safety of the entire country depended on his efforts. He sacrificed his comfort and time with his loved ones to make sure the land would be safe for future generations.

Lessons from Yu the Great: Hard Work, Leadership, and Responsibility

Yu's story teaches us many important lessons that are still valuable today. One of the biggest lessons is about the importance of hard work. Yu didn't solve the problem overnight—he worked for thirteen years, day and night, until the flood was under control. His story shows that patience and perseverance are essential when tackling big challenges.

Another lesson from Yu the Great is about leadership. A true leader, like Yu, doesn't just give orders—he works alongside others, inspires them, and never gives up, even when things get tough. Yu's actions show us that a good leader cares about others and works for the greater good.

Yu's story is also about responsibility. He could have chosen to return home and live a quiet life with his family, but instead, he took on the enormous task of saving the land from the flood. Yu teaches us that taking responsibility for problems—even when they seem overwhelming—makes a difference. Each of us can make the world a better place by doing our part, just as Yu did.

A Hero Who Built a Legacy

Because of Yu's hard work, the canals and dams he built saved countless lives and allowed the land to flourish once again. The crops began to grow, rivers flowed peacefully, and people could rebuild their homes and villages. Yu the Great's achievements were so remarkable that the people of China named him their leader, and he became the founder of the Xia Dynasty, the first dynasty in Chinese history.

Even today, Yu the Great is remembered as a hero. His story reminds us that no matter how big the challenge, with hard work, leadership, and a sense of responsibility, we can overcome any obstacle. Yu didn't just fight the flood—he taught people how to live in harmony with nature, setting an example for future generations.

The next time you face a challenge, big or small, think of Yu the Great. He teaches us that problems can be solved with patience, teamwork, and smart thinking. Whether you're working on a school project, helping a friend, or finding a solution to a problem at home, you can make a difference—just like Yu did.

And remember, you don't need to tame a flood to be a hero. You can be a hero by taking responsibility, leading with kindness, and working hard to make things better, even in small ways. Yu the Great shows us that the greatest heroes are those who care for others and never give up, no matter how hard the journey may be.

So, as you explore the world of Chinese legends, keep Yu's lessons in mind. Be brave, be kind, and be responsible—and who knows? Maybe one day, you'll create your own story of greatness!

CHAPTER 12: THE STORY OF HOU YI - THE ARCHER WHO SHOT DOWN NINE SUNS

A long, long time ago, ancient China had not one, but ten suns in the sky. These ten suns were brothers who lived high in the heavens. They took turns rising each day, bringing light and warmth to the world. Each sun would shine on a different day, making sure the land and rivers had just the right amount of sunlight.

But one day, the ten brothers grew restless. They decided it would be fun to rise into the sky all at once! The moment they did, the world became unbearably hot. Rivers dried up, crops withered, and animals had no place to hide from the scorching heat. Even the people couldn't find relief, and it seemed like everything would soon be destroyed by the blazing suns.

No one knew what to do. The people prayed to the gods, begging for help. It seemed that no one could stop the suns—until a hero named Hou Yi stepped forward.

How Hou Yi's Skill Saved the Earth

Hou Yi was a famous archer, known throughout the land for his unmatched skill with the bow and arrow. He was not only strong but also brave and determined to save the earth. When the gods saw how desperate the people were, they gave Hou Yi a magical bow and a quiver of enchanted arrows. With these tools, Hou Yi would have the power to stop the ten suns.

Hou Yi climbed to the top of the highest mountain, where he could see all ten suns shining fiercely in the sky. He knew that if he didn't act quickly, the world would be lost. He pulled out his first arrow, aimed carefully, and let it fly.

With a sharp whistle, the arrow soared through the sky and struck one of the suns. The sun flickered and then fell from the sky, disappearing over the horizon. The temperature cooled slightly, but it was still too hot. Hou Yi knew he had to shoot down more suns to save the earth.

One by one, Hou Yi shot down the suns, each time making the world a little cooler. The rivers began to flow again, the crops perked up, and animals returned to their homes. But soon, only one sun remained in the sky. Hou Yi realized that if he shot down the last sun, the world would be covered in darkness forever.

So, with great wisdom, Hou Yi spared the final sun. He let it shine gently over the land, knowing that the people needed both light and warmth to survive.

Lessons from Hou Yi: Heroism, Balance, and Sacrifice

Hou Yi's story is about more than just bravery. It teaches us many important lessons about balance, sacrifice, and what it means to be a hero.

First, Hou Yi showed incredible courage by facing a challenge that seemed impossible. Even though he was just one man, he didn't hesitate to take action when the world needed him. This teaches us that heroes aren't always the strongest or the biggest—they are the ones who act bravely when it matters most.

Hou Yi also teaches us about balance. He could have shot down all ten suns, but he realized that the earth needed light to survive. This reminds us that too much of anything—even something good—can be harmful. Life needs balance, just like the world needs both day and night.

Finally, Hou Yi's sacrifice shows us the importance of putting others before ourselves. After saving the earth, Hou Yi could have been celebrated as a hero. But instead of resting, he continued to use his skills to help others. In some versions of the story, Hou Yi even gives up his immortality for the sake of love, choosing to live as a mortal with his wife, Chang'e. His actions remind us that true heroism comes from selflessness and compassion.

Hou Yi's story has been told for generations in China, inspiring children and adults alike. He is remembered as a hero who saved the earth and restored balance to the world. His bravery and wisdom teach us that even in the face of overwhelming challenges, we can find solutions if we are willing to act with courage and thoughtfulness.

Today, the story of Hou Yi is still celebrated during festivals and holidays, reminding people to appreciate the sun that shines above them and the balance that makes life possible. Whenever you see the sun rising in the morning, you can think of Hou Yi and the moment he chose to save the earth—not by destroying all the suns, but by finding the right balance between light and darkness.

And who knows? Maybe one day, when you face a challenge of your own, you'll remember the story of Hou Yi and find the courage to act with bravery, wisdom, and kindness—just like the great archer who shot down nine suns.

CHAPTER 13: THE TALE OF ZAO SHEN - THE KITCHEN GOD

A long time ago, in ancient China, people believed that every household had a special guardian—Zao Shen, the Kitchen God. Unlike mighty warriors or fierce dragons, Zao Shen's job was a little different but just as important. He watched over the everyday lives of families, making sure that their homes were peaceful, their meals were nourishing, and their hearts were full of gratitude.

Zao Shen didn't live in the heavens like the other gods. He lived right in the kitchen of every home, where families cooked their meals and gathered to eat. In Chinese culture, the kitchen is more than just a place to make food—it's the heart of the household, where people connect, share stories, and show care for one another. This made Zao Shen's role very special because he was believed to protect and guide families in their daily lives.

But Zao Shen didn't just sit quietly in the kitchen. He observed everything that happened—the good and the bad. If a family worked together, treated each other with kindness, and prepared meals with love, Zao Shen was pleased. But if there were arguments, dishonesty, or laziness, Zao Shen noticed that, too. He kept a record of everything, ready to report back to the Jade Emperor, the ruler of heaven.

The Ritual of Sending Zao Shen's Spirit to Heaven on New Year's Eve

Every year, on New Year's Eve, something exciting happened. Families believed that Zao Shen traveled to the heavens to give a report on everything he had seen in the household throughout the year. The Jade Emperor would listen carefully to Zao Shen's report, and based on what he heard, he would decide whether the family deserved blessings or needed to work on becoming better in the new year.

So, as New Year's Eve approached, families prepared for Zao Shen's journey. They wanted to make sure that he delivered a positive report! To keep Zao Shen happy, families would clean their homes from top to bottom, showing that they were ready for a fresh start.

One of the most important parts of the New Year's Eve ritual was the offering made to Zao Shen. Families would prepare sweet, sticky treats, like malt sugar cakes, and place them on the altar next to the stove. Why? The sweets were said to "sweeten" Zao Shen's mouth—so when he spoke to the Jade Emperor, he would only have kind things to say! Some families even believed that the sticky cakes would keep Zao Shen's mouth too full to mention anything negative.

When everything was ready, families would light incense and say a prayer of gratitude to Zao Shen for watching over their home. Then, they would burn a special paper image of the Kitchen God, symbolically sending his spirit to the heavens.

But don't worry—Zao Shen didn't stay in the heavens for long. On the first day of the new year, his spirit returned to the household, ready to watch over the family for another year. Families welcomed him back with a fresh paper image, hung proudly near the kitchen stove, so Zao Shen would feel at home once again.

Lessons from Zao Shen: Honesty, Home, and Gratitude

Zao Shen's story may be about a small, humble kitchen, but the lessons it teaches are big and meaningful. One of the most important things we learn from Zao Shen is honesty. Just like Zao Shen observed everything in the kitchen, the story reminds us that our actions matter, whether someone is watching or not. It teaches us that it's important to do the right thing—not just to impress others, but because it's the right thing to do.

Another lesson from Zao Shen's story is about the importance of home and family. The kitchen is where people gather to share meals, stories, and moments of joy. Zao Shen's presence reminds us to care for one another and to make our homes places of love, respect, and kindness. When families work together and support each other, it creates a peaceful, happy home.

Finally, gratitude is at the heart of Zao Shen's story. Every year, families took time to say thank you to the Kitchen God and reflect on the blessings they had received. This teaches us the importance of being grateful for what we have—whether it's the food on our table, the people we love, or the small moments of happiness that make life special.

Even today, many families in China and other parts of the world celebrate the Kitchen God during the Lunar New Year. It's a time to reflect on the past year, make new goals, and show gratitude for the blessings of family and home. And while not everyone believes in Zao Shen anymore, his story lives on, reminding people of the importance of honesty, kindness, and gratitude.

The next time you sit down for a family meal or help in the kitchen, think of Zao Shen, the Kitchen God who quietly watches over every home. How would your actions make Zao Shen feel? Would he be proud to report your kindness and hard work to the Jade Emperor?

Through the story of Zao Shen, we learn that every small action—like sharing a meal, being kind to a family member, or saying thank you—matters. And just like the Kitchen God keeps watch over the heart of the home, we, too, can look out for those around us, making our homes and communities places of warmth and care.

So, as you enjoy your next meal, take a moment to think about what you're grateful for. Whether it's your family, your friends, or even just the food on your plate, a little bit of gratitude goes a long way. And who knows—maybe Zao Shen is still watching, ready to bring good fortune to those who live with kindness and joy!

CHAPTER 14: THE LEGEND OF THE BUTTERFLY LOVERS - A TALE OF TRAGIC LOVE

Long ago, in ancient China, there lived a young woman named Zhu Yingtai. Zhu was kind and curious, with a heart full of dreams. But in her time, girls weren't allowed to go to school. Zhu Yingtai, however, was determined to learn, so she came up with a clever plan. She dressed as a boy and set off to study in a distant academy, disguising her true identity so she could follow her dream.

At the academy, Zhu met Liang Shanbo, a bright young man with a gentle soul. The two students quickly became best friends. They studied together, laughed together, and shared many adventures. But as time passed, Zhu Yingtai's feelings for Liang Shanbo grew deeper. She wasn't just his friend—she had fallen in love with him.

Sadly, Liang Shanbo didn't know that Zhu Yingtai was really a girl. He thought they were simply two close friends, bound by loyalty and trust. As the seasons changed, Zhu's heart grew heavier. She knew that one day, her disguise would be discovered. But how would Liang Shanbo feel when he learned the truth?

The Power of Love That Transcends Life and Death

After three years of studying together, it was time for Zhu Yingtai to return home. She still couldn't bring herself to tell Liang Shanbo who she really was. Before she left, she gave him a clue—she hinted that she would love for them to meet again one day, not as friends, but as something more. Liang Shanbo, however, didn't understand her meaning right away.

It wasn't until much later, when Liang Shanbo visited Zhu's home, that the truth was finally revealed. When he saw Zhu dressed in her beautiful robes, not as a boy but as herself, he realized that she had been the love of his life all along. His heart filled with joy, but that joy was short-lived—there was terrible news waiting for him.

Zhu's family had already arranged for her to marry another man. Though Zhu and Liang's love for each other was pure and true, her family's decision could not be undone. Liang Shanbo's heart was shattered. The thought of losing Zhu was too much for him to bear. Unable to live without her, Liang Shanbo fell gravely ill and soon passed away, his spirit longing for the love he could never have.

When Zhu Yingtai heard the news of Liang's death, she was devastated. On the day of her wedding, she went to visit Liang Shanbo's tomb, dressed in her bridal gown. Standing by his grave, Zhu prayed with all her heart, wishing that they could be together in some way, even if not in this life. Her love for Liang Shanbo was so powerful that the ground began to tremble, and the tomb opened up.

Without hesitation, Zhu Yingtai leapt into the tomb, joining her beloved in death. In that moment, something miraculous happened—two beautiful butterflies emerged from the tomb, fluttering together into the sky. The two lovers, reunited at last, had transformed into butterflies, free to fly wherever they wished. In the form of butterflies, their love was no longer bound by life, death, or earthly rules.

Lessons from the Butterfly Lovers: Freedom, Love, and Acceptance

The story of Zhu Yingtai and Liang Shanbo is often called the "Chinese Romeo and Juliet," but it offers its own unique lessons about love, freedom, and acceptance. Their tale teaches us that true love cannot be stopped—not by rules, not by distance, and not even by death. It shows us that love is powerful enough to transcend all boundaries and that when two hearts are truly connected, they will always find a way to be together.

The transformation of the two lovers into butterflies carries deep meaning. Butterflies are a symbol of freedom and change. Just as a caterpillar transforms into a butterfly, Zhu and Liang's love transformed them, setting them free from the limitations of the world. Their spirits were no longer bound by family expectations or earthly struggles—they were free to fly together forever.

This story also teaches us about acceptance and letting go. Though Zhu and Liang faced many obstacles in their lives, their love endured. And even when it seemed like everything was lost, their transformation into butterflies reminds us that every ending can be a new beginning. Love has the power to transform even the saddest moments into something beautiful.

Through the legend of the Butterfly Lovers, we learn that it's okay to follow our hearts, even when the path is difficult. True love requires patience and courage, just like Zhu Yingtai showed when she leapt into Liang's tomb, trusting that they would find a way to be together.

The Legacy of the Butterfly Lovers

The story of the Butterfly Lovers has been told for centuries, inspiring plays, songs, and dances across China. Even today, their tale continues to capture the hearts of people all over the world. During the spring, when butterflies flutter through gardens and fields, people often remember Zhu Yingtai and Liang Shanbo, imagining their love story flying with the wind.

This story is also celebrated in Chinese opera and music, reminding people of the importance of love, freedom, and loyalty. Many couples visit shrines and temples dedicated to the Butterfly Lovers, offering prayers for lasting love and happiness.

So, the next time you see two butterflies dancing in the air, think of Zhu Yingtai and Liang Shanbo. Remember that love, just like butterflies, is delicate but strong, capable of soaring through any challenge. And if you ever face difficulties in your own life, remember the lesson of the Butterfly Lovers—even in the hardest times, love and hope will always find a way to shine through.

CHAPTER 15: THE STORY OF THE BAMBOO CUTTER - THE TALE OF KAGUYA

Long ago, deep in the heart of a quiet forest, there lived an old bamboo cutter and his wife. Every day, the bamboo cutter went into the forest, carefully slicing down tall bamboo stalks to sell. One day, something extraordinary happened. As he was working, the old man noticed a faint glow coming from one of the bamboo stalks. Curious, he cut it open, and to his amazement, inside the glowing bamboo, he found a tiny, beautiful girl no bigger than his hand.

The old couple had no children, so they took the tiny girl home, believing she was a gift from the heavens. As soon as they brought her into their home, the little girl magically grew into a normal-sized baby. Overjoyed, the bamboo cutter and his wife named her Kaguya, which means "shining light," because of how she had come to them, glowing inside the bamboo.

Kaguya was no ordinary girl. She was as beautiful as the moon and as graceful as a spring breeze. As she grew, her beauty became even more radiant, and soon, news of the mysterious girl spread across the land. Suitors and noblemen traveled from far and wide to ask for her hand in marriage, but Kaguya was kind but distant. She loved her adoptive parents dearly but didn't seem to belong entirely to the world of humans. There was always a spark of mystery about her, as if her heart were connected to something far beyond the earth.

Kaguya's Magical Journey to the Moon

Many suitors tried to win Kaguya's heart, but she refused them all, setting them impossible tasks. One nobleman was asked to find the Jewel of the Dragon King's Palace beneath the sea, while another was told to bring her a branch of silver from a distant mountain. One by one, the suitors failed, proving they were not worthy of her. Kaguya remained alone, but not sad—there was a secret longing in her heart.

One night, during the full moon, Kaguya stood outside her home, gazing up at the glowing sky. Her parents noticed tears in her eyes and asked her what was troubling her. It was then that Kaguya revealed the truth.

"I am not from this world," she said softly. "I come from the moon, and soon, the time will come for me to return." The bamboo cutter and his wife were heartbroken. They loved Kaguya as their daughter and could not bear the thought of losing her. Kaguya, too, was filled with sorrow, for she had come to love her life on Earth.

As the full moon approached, a golden chariot descended from the sky, sent by the moon people to bring Kaguya back to her true home. Kaguya's parents tried to hold on to her, but they knew they couldn't stop destiny. With tears in her eyes, Kaguya bid farewell to the kind couple who had taken her in and loved her as their own. She gave them a letter and a special gift—a bottle of the Elixir of Immortality, which she hoped would bring them comfort after she was gone.

Kaguya stepped into the glowing chariot, and with one final glance at the Earth she had come to love, she rose into the night sky, disappearing into the soft glow of the moon. The bamboo cutter and his wife watched her until she was out of sight, their hearts heavy with both sadness and gratitude.

Lessons from Kaguya: Magic, Mystery, and Destiny

The tale of Kaguya teaches us many valuable lessons about the wonders of life, the magic of kindness, and the importance of accepting what we cannot change. Though Kaguya's life on Earth was brief, she brought joy and love to those around her. Her story reminds us that even the smallest moments with those we love can leave a lasting impact.

One of the most powerful lessons in Kaguya's story is accepting destiny with grace. Even though Kaguya didn't want to leave her life on Earth, she understood that some things are beyond our control. Her return to the moon reminds us that life is full of changes, and sometimes, we must let go of what we hold dear.

Kaguya's story is also about the beauty of mystery and magic. Not everything in life can be explained, and that's what makes it so magical. Just like the moon shines brightly in the night sky, Kaguya's story reminds us to find wonder in the world around us, even in the moments that seem sad or difficult.

The Elixir of Immortality that Kaguya left behind for her parents symbolizes the eternal power of love and memory. Even though Kaguya returned to the moon, her love for her earthly parents remained with them forever, showing that love transcends time and distance.

The Legacy of Kaguya

The tale of Kaguya, also known as "The Tale of the Bamboo Cutter," is one of the oldest legends in Chinese and Japanese storytelling. It has inspired countless stories, plays, and even movies, reminding people to embrace life's mysteries and cherish the people they love.

To this day, when people look at the moon, some say they can see the outline of Kaguya, watching over the Earth she once called home. Her story is especially remembered during Mid-Autumn Festival celebrations, when people gather to admire the full moon and share mooncakes with family and friends.

So, the next time you look up at the moon, think of Kaguya and her magical journey. Remember that life is full of wonder, even when things don't go the way we expect. And just like Kaguya's love for her parents, the bonds we share with others can last forever, no matter where life takes us. After all, the moon always shines down, even on the darkest nights—just like love and memories stay with us, lighting up our hearts.

CHAPTER 16: THE STORY OF THE CARP THAT BECAME A DRAGON

◆◇◇◉◇◇◆

Long ago, in a sparkling river nestled between towering mountains, there lived a small carp. The carp was no ordinary fish—it was filled with dreams of greatness. Day by day, it watched the waters flow past, yearning to reach the source of the river at the top of the great waterfall. The carp heard an ancient legend: any fish that could swim all the way upstream and leap over the waterfall would be transformed into a mighty dragon.

Though many laughed at the idea, the little carp refused to give up its dream. It knew the journey would be tough, but it was determined to try. One bright morning, the carp set off, swimming against the current. The river was filled with challenges— swift currents pushed the carp backward, and sharp rocks threatened to block its way.

Some of the bigger fish mocked the carp. "You'll never make it up the waterfall," they sneered. But the small carp kept swimming, saying to itself, "I may be small, but I am strong in spirit!" Every time the current pushed it back, the carp swam harder. It dodged rocks, jumped over rapids, and swam past creatures much larger than itself.

At last, the carp reached the base of the great waterfall. It looked up, and the water thundered down like a giant curtain of silver. The carp knew that this would be the hardest part of the journey. Many fish had tried to leap over the waterfall before, but none had ever succeeded.

With a burst of energy, the little carp leaped into the rushing water. It jumped once—only to fall back down. It jumped again, only to be swept away by the force of the waterfall. But the carp refused to give up. With each attempt, it grew stronger and more determined.

Finally, after what seemed like countless tries, the carp made one last mighty leap. It soared through the spray, higher and higher, until it reached the top of the waterfall. And in that moment, something incredible happened.

The heavens rumbled, and a dazzling light surrounded the little carp. Its scales shimmered like gold, and its small body began to grow and change. The carp transformed into a majestic dragon, with gleaming horns, powerful wings, and a long, flowing tail. The new dragon roared with joy, swirling through the clouds and soaring across the sky. It had achieved its dream—and in doing so, it became a symbol of transformation and triumph.

The Symbolism of Perseverance and Transformation in Chinese Folklore

The story of the carp that became a dragon has been told for centuries in Chinese folklore. It is a tale about transformation, perseverance, and never giving up, no matter how hard the challenge. The small carp represents anyone with a big dream, while the rushing river and the waterfall symbolize the obstacles that stand in the way.

In Chinese culture, dragons are powerful creatures that symbolize strength, luck, and success. The transformation of the carp into a dragon reminds us that even the smallest of us can achieve great things if we work hard and stay determined. The journey of the carp is also a lesson about personal growth. Sometimes, we must go through tough times and face difficult challenges before we can become the best versions of ourselves.

This legend is often used to encourage students, athletes, and anyone working toward a goal. It shows that true success comes from hard work and persistence, even when things seem impossible. Just like the carp that swam upstream, we all have the potential to achieve something amazing if we believe in ourselves and keep trying.

Lessons from the Carp: Determination, Hard Work, and Success

The story of the carp teaches us many important lessons that we can use in our own lives:

1. Determination is Key: The little carp never gave up, even when the waterfall seemed impossible to climb. It teaches us that if we want to achieve something, we have to keep going, no matter how hard it gets.

2. Hard Work Pays Off: Just like the carp's repeated attempts made it stronger, the effort we put into our goals helps us grow and learn. Each step, even a small one, brings us closer to success.

3. Success Comes from Within: The carp may have started as a small, ordinary fish, but it had a powerful spirit. The legend reminds us that true strength comes from within, and that greatness is not about size or appearance but about heart and determination.

4. Embrace Transformation: Just as the carp transformed into a dragon, we can also change and grow through our experiences. Every challenge we

face helps us become stronger, wiser, and more prepared for what's ahead.

The Legacy of the Carp and the Dragon

The story of the carp's transformation into a dragon is celebrated in many ways in Chinese culture. It serves as a symbol of success and is often associated with achievements in education, career, and personal growth. People often say, "May you leap over the dragon's gate," as a way of wishing someone good luck and success in their journey.

During the annual Dragon Boat Festival, brightly decorated boats shaped like dragons race along rivers, celebrating the power and energy of the dragon. The festival also reminds people of the importance of working together, just as the carp worked with the river and its currents to achieve its dream.

This legend continues to inspire people of all ages, encouraging them to face challenges with courage and determination. Whenever life feels tough, just remember the little carp—keep swimming, keep trying, and one day, you too might find yourself soaring like a dragon.

So, the next time you feel like giving up, think of the small carp standing at the base of the waterfall. With patience, effort, and belief in yourself, you can conquer even the greatest challenges—and who knows, you might just discover your own dragon waiting within you!

CHAPTER 17: THE LEGEND OF SUN AND MOON CAKES - A HIDDEN MESSAGE

✦ ◇◇◉◇◇ ✦

Long ago, in ancient China, people lived under the rule of a cruel emperor who treated his subjects unfairly. Life was hard for many, and the people longed for freedom. But how could they fight against such a powerful emperor? The answer came in the form of a clever plan—and some delicious moon cakes.

During the Mid-Autumn Festival, people would exchange moon cakes, round pastries filled with sweet fillings like lotus seed paste or red bean paste. These cakes were more than just treats; they held a secret. A group of rebels, who wanted to free the people from the emperor's harsh rule, came up with an idea: they would hide messages inside the moon cakes, spreading the word about their plan for a rebellion.

Inside each moon cake was a small piece of paper with instructions. The messages told people to rise up against the emperor on the night of the next full moon. Because the moon cakes were part of the festival traditions, the emperor's guards didn't suspect a thing. The rebels handed out the cakes across the land, and soon, the message reached every corner of the empire.

On the night of the full moon, the people rose together in unity, following the instructions hidden inside the moon cakes. Their plan worked! The emperor was overthrown, and the people celebrated their freedom. Ever since that day, moon cakes have been more than just a sweet treat—they are a symbol of unity, hope, and freedom.

The Traditions of Eating Moon Cakes During Festivals

Today, the legend of the moon cakes lives on through the Mid-Autumn Festival, also called the Moon Festival. Every year, families come together to eat moon cakes and celebrate under the bright, full moon. The round shape of the cakes represents unity and togetherness, reminding everyone of the importance of family and community.

During the festival, children carry colorful lanterns and listen to stories about the moon and the stars. The festival is also connected to the legend of Chang'e, the Moon Goddess, who flew to the moon and now watches over the Earth from the night sky. People gather to admire the moon, share stories, and enjoy delicious moon cakes with their loved ones.

Moon cakes come in many flavors, with fillings like sweet red bean paste, nuts, and even salted egg yolks to represent the moon. Each bite of a moon cake is a reminder of the festival's history and the legends passed down through generations. Families often give moon cakes as gifts, symbolizing love and respect for one another.

Lessons from the Moon Cake Legend: Unity, Freedom, and Tradition

The story of the moon cakes teaches us many important lessons. First, it shows the power of unity. Just like the rebels worked together to achieve their goal, we can accomplish great things when we come together with a common purpose. Whether it's standing up for what is right or helping someone in need, unity makes us stronger.

The legend also reminds us about the value of freedom. The people in the story fought bravely to free themselves from the emperor's rule. Freedom is a gift that should be cherished, and it's important to remember the courage of those who stood up for what they believed in.

Finally, the story of the moon cakes teaches us about tradition. Festivals like the Mid-Autumn Festival are not just celebrations—they are a way to connect with our history and pass down stories from one generation to the next. By celebrating traditions, we honor our ancestors and keep their wisdom alive.

So, the next time you enjoy a moon cake during the Mid-Autumn Festival, think about the hidden messages that once helped start a rebellion. Remember the power of unity, the importance of freedom, and the joy of sharing traditions with those around you. And who knows—maybe there's a little bit of magic in every moon cake!

CHAPTER 18: THE LEGEND OF THE RED THREAD OF FATE - INVISIBLE CONNECTIONS

———————— ✦ ◇◇◉◇◇ ✦ ————————

A long, long time ago, in ancient China, there was a legend about an invisible red thread that connected people. This thread was no ordinary string—it was a magical thread of fate, binding together two people who were destined to meet. No matter how far apart they lived or how different their lives were, the thread would eventually bring them together.

The legend says that the red thread is tied to a person's ankle or finger by the gods at the moment they are born. As the years go by, the thread may twist and tangle, but it will never break. The two people connected by the thread might meet as friends, family members, or even soulmates. Sometimes they might not meet until many years later, but they are always meant to find each other in the end.

The story goes that one day, a boy asked an old matchmaker how love and friendships were formed. The matchmaker, a wise old man with a bag of red thread, explained the magic of the invisible connections. "Even though you can't see it," the matchmaker said, "the red thread guides your heart and brings you to the people who matter most." The boy was amazed, wondering where his own thread would lead him one day.

The Power of Fate and Destiny in Chinese Beliefs

The red thread of fate is not just a story about love—it is a symbol of fate and destiny in Chinese culture. Many believe that the people we meet in life are not by chance, but are meant to be a part of our journey. Whether it's a friend who helps us through tough times, a teacher who guides us, or someone who makes us laugh, the red thread pulls these people into our lives at just the right moment.

In Chinese tradition, the red thread reminds us that some things in life are beyond our control. No matter how much we plan or worry, fate will play a role in our journey. But this doesn't mean we should sit and wait for things to happen. Instead, the red thread teaches us to trust that the right people will come into our lives when the time is right.

Many people in China still believe in the idea of fate, especially when it comes to friendships and love. Parents might tell their children that everyone has a red thread connecting them to someone special, giving them hope and excitement about the future. Couples sometimes give each other gifts tied with red thread, symbolizing their bond and destiny.

Lessons from the Red Thread: Patience, Trust, and Destiny

The legend of the red thread teaches us many important lessons. First, it reminds us to be patient. Just like a tangled thread takes time to unravel, finding the people we are meant to meet can take time. Sometimes, we might feel lonely or frustrated, but the red thread teaches us to trust that good things will come.

Trust is another lesson from the red thread. Even when we can't see it, the thread is always there, silently connecting us to the right people. This teaches us to have faith in the journey, even when things don't happen the way we expect. Life might have twists and turns, but the red thread shows us that everything happens for a reason.

Finally, the red thread helps us understand the idea of destiny. It teaches us that every friendship, every relationship, and every encounter matters. Even if someone is only in our life for a short time, they play a role in our story. Every twist in the thread is part of the adventure.

A Story of Two Friends Brought Together by the Red Thread

Once, there were two children named Mei and Tao who lived in different villages, far from each other. One loved to write stories, and the other dreamed of becoming an artist. Though they didn't know it, the red thread of fate had already connected them.

One day, Tao's family moved to Mei's village, and the two children met at a market. Mei showed Tao her favorite books, and Tao gave Mei a small drawing as a gift. From that moment on, the two became best friends, spending hours creating storybooks filled with drawings and adventures.

Years later, when they were older, they opened a bookstore and art studio together, sharing their creativity with the world. Mei and Tao often laughed about how lucky they were to have found each other, but deep down, they knew it wasn't luck—it was the magic of the red thread, guiding them to the friendship they were always meant to have.

The legend of the red thread teaches us that even when we feel lost or alone, we are never truly disconnected. The thread winds through our lives, weaving together people, places, and experiences that shape who we are. Every friendship, every act of kindness, and every challenge is part of the journey, and the people we meet along the way are part of our story.

So, the next time you make a new friend or meet someone special, imagine the invisible red thread that brought you together. And remember—just like Mei and Tao, the right people will find their way into your life, even if it takes a little time.

The red thread of fate is a reminder that we are all connected by love, friendship, and hope. It teaches us to trust the journey, be patient with life's twists and turns, and embrace the magic of meeting the people we were always meant to know.

CHAPTER 19: FESTIVALS AND CELEBRATIONS - HONORING THE LEGENDS

―――――◆◇◇◉◇◇◆―――――

China's festivals are magical times when communities come together to celebrate legends, traditions, and heroes. These festivals not only honor the past but also help families and friends create joyful memories. Two of the most exciting and colorful festivals are the Lantern Festival and the Dragon Boat Festival. These celebrations are rooted in Chinese history and tell stories that have been passed down for centuries.

The Lantern Festival, celebrated on the 15th day of the Lunar New Year, is like a grand finale to the Chinese New Year celebrations. Families gather to light lanterns of all shapes, sizes, and colors, creating a glowing sea of lights. According to legend, lighting lanterns helps guide spirits back to the heavens and symbolizes hope and brightness for the year ahead. Children often carry animal-shaped lanterns, while adults write wishes and riddles on theirs. The festival also honors Zao Shen, the Kitchen God, and celebrates unity and the renewal of life.

The Dragon Boat Festival is another vibrant celebration held in honor of the poet Qu Yuan, who gave his life for his country. Legend says that after Qu Yuan drowned in a river, the villagers raced in boats to save him. Today, people honor his bravery with thrilling dragon boat races, colorful parades, and zongzi, a special rice dumpling wrapped in bamboo leaves. The races are not only exciting to watch but also symbolize the strength of community and teamwork. The rhythm of the paddlers rowing to the beat of drums creates an unforgettable atmosphere.

How Communities Keep Their Legends Alive With Dance, Music, and Food

Chinese festivals are not just about decorations and races—they are filled with dances, music, and delicious foods that bring the legends to life. Lion dances are a must-see during festivals, with performers wearing giant lion costumes and dancing to the rhythm of drums and cymbals. According to legend, the lion's dance scares away evil spirits and brings good luck to the community. Children and adults cheer and clap as the colorful lions leap and twirl through the streets.

Music also plays a big part in these celebrations. Traditional instruments like drums, gongs, and flutes fill the air with joyful sounds. Folk songs are sung to honor legendary heroes, and each melody tells a story about the bravery, kindness, or wisdom of the past. Some festivals even include storytelling sessions where elders share ancient legends with children, keeping the stories alive for future generations.

Food, of course, is at the heart of every celebration! During the Lantern Festival, people enjoy tangyuan, sweet glutinous rice balls, symbolizing unity and family togetherness. At the Dragon Boat Festival, zongzi is shared with friends and neighbors, reminding everyone of the importance of tradition and kindness. Festival foods not only taste delicious but are also filled with meaning. Each dish tells a story, connecting the people who prepare and share it to the legends of the past.

What Festivals Teach Us: Gratitude, Joy, and Cultural Pride

Festivals are not only about fun and feasting—they also teach important lessons about gratitude, joy, and pride in one's culture. The legends celebrated during these festivals remind people to be thankful for the heroes and traditions that have shaped their lives. The Lantern Festival teaches gratitude for new beginnings and the light that guides us forward. The Dragon Boat Festival reminds us to be grateful for the sacrifices made by those who came before us, like Qu Yuan.

Joy is another important lesson of these celebrations. Festivals are times to set aside worries and celebrate life with laughter, music, and dance. They bring communities together, showing that happiness is best when shared with others. Whether it's children running with lanterns or families enjoying festival meals, these joyful moments remind everyone of the beauty of togetherness.

Finally, festivals inspire pride in one's heritage and traditions. Through these celebrations, people connect with their roots, learning about the stories, values, and customs passed down from their ancestors. Cultural pride helps people understand who they are and where they come from, fostering a sense of belonging and unity. For children, participating in these festivals is a chance to feel proud of their culture and share it with friends from different backgrounds.

At the heart of every Chinese festival is a deep connection to the past, the present, and the future. The stories and traditions celebrated during these times remind us of the heroes and values that shape our lives. Through dance, music, food, and fun, these festivals keep legends alive, passing their wisdom to each new generation.

Whether it's the glowing lanterns lighting up the night sky or the splash of dragon boats racing down a river, each celebration is a reminder that legends live on in our hearts and communities. The joy, gratitude, and pride shared during these festivals help people connect with one another, fostering unity and happiness.

So, the next time you see a glowing lantern or hear the beat of a drum during a festival, remember the legends that inspire these celebrations. And who knows—maybe one day, you'll create your own traditions and stories to pass down, becoming part of the magical world of legends that keeps our cultures alive!

CONCLUSION:
CREATE YOUR OWN CHINESE LEGEND!

---◆◇◎◇◆---

Chinese legends have been told for thousands of years, and they still captivate our imaginations today. Why do these stories continue to inspire so many people across generations? The answer lies in the way these legends combine adventure, magic, and important life lessons. Each tale carries values like kindness, bravery, respect, and wisdom—qualities that are just as important now as they were in ancient times.

When you read the story of the Monkey King learning to control his wild nature or Chang'e flying to the moon, you feel connected to characters from a distant time who still face challenges similar to ours. These stories remind us to dream big, be kind, and never give up, no matter how difficult things get. Legends are more than just entertainment—they teach us how to live, how to grow, and how to make the world a better place.

Every generation has added its own voice to these legends, keeping them alive and relevant. Now it's your turn! Just like ancient storytellers, you have the power to create your own legends and share them with the world.

How to Craft Your Own Stories Using Chinese Themes and Characters

Creating your own Chinese legend is easier than you might think! Every great legend starts with imagination. Think about the elements you love from the stories you've read—maybe it's a magical dragon, a clever trickster, or a brave hero like Mulan. You can use these characters or themes as inspiration to build your very own story.

Here are a few fun ideas to get you started:

- Create a New Dragon Hero: Imagine a dragon that controls the wind and embarks on a mission to restore peace between the heavens and the earth.
- Invent a Festival: What if your legend explains how a brand-new festival came to be? Maybe it celebrates a brave child who saved their village from a terrible monster!
- Tell the Story of a Magical Object: Just like the Monkey King's magical staff, your story could feature an enchanted item with extraordinary powers.

You can also mix traditional themes with new ideas. Maybe your character is a modern-day kid who discovers they are connected to an ancient legend and goes on an adventure to fulfill their destiny. You can draw inspiration from Chinese symbols, like dragons (which represent strength), the moon (which symbolizes change), or the red thread of fate (which connects people who are destined to meet). The possibilities are endless!

The Power of Storytelling: Passing Traditions from One Generation to the Next

Storytelling has been one of the most important ways people have shared knowledge, wisdom, and values across generations. In ancient China, stories weren't just for fun—they were a way to teach children about their history, culture, and traditions. By telling these stories to the next generation, families ensured that their values and beliefs would never be forgotten.

When you write or tell your own stories, you're becoming part of a tradition that stretches back thousands of years. Storytelling connects us to our ancestors and helps us understand who we are. And the best part is, you can use stories to pass on important lessons to others! Whether you share a story about courage, friendship, or kindness, your words have the power to inspire people just like the legends of the past.

As you've seen throughout this book, Chinese legends are filled with adventure, magic, and meaning. Now it's your turn to become a storyteller! Don't worry if your story isn't perfect at first—even the greatest legends began as simple ideas. The most important thing is to have fun and let your imagination soar.

So, grab a notebook or sit down with a friend, and start dreaming up your own Chinese legend. Will your story feature a heroic dragon flying through the skies? Or maybe a clever trickster who teaches everyone a lesson about kindness? No matter what you choose, remember that there's no limit to where your imagination can take you.

Just like a dragon soaring through the clouds or a hero braving an impossible challenge, your creativity knows no bounds. Who knows? Maybe one day, your story will be told for generations to come, inspiring others just as these legends have inspired you.

Now, it's time to begin your storytelling adventure. Dream big, write boldly, and let your imagination fly like a dragon! Your legend awaits!

BONUS SECTION: FUN ACTIVITIES INSPIRED BY CHINESE LEGENDS

Welcome to the Bonus Section! Now that you've read about brave heroes, clever tricksters, and magical creatures, it's time to have some fun and let your creativity shine. This section is packed with activities inspired by the stories in this book. Grab your art supplies, pens, and paper—let's jump into the world of Chinese legends and create something amazing!

Create Your Own Dragon Mask: Design a Dragon Mask with Colors and Meaning

In Chinese culture, dragons are powerful symbols of strength, good luck, and protection. Now it's your turn to create your very own dragon mask! When making your mask, think about what kind of dragon it represents. Is it a water dragon swimming through rivers or a fire-breathing dragon soaring through the skies?

What You'll Need:

- A large piece of paper or cardboard
- Markers, crayons, or paint
- Scissors (ask an adult for help!)
- String or elastic to tie the mask
- Feathers, glitter, or anything else to decorate

Steps:

- Draw the shape of your dragon's face. Is it long and serpentine, like the traditional Chinese dragon? Or does it have a fierce snout and sharp horns?
- Color your dragon mask. Use bright colors like red and gold to symbolize good luck, or blue and green for a water dragon.
- Add special details. Glue on feathers for eyebrows or use glitter for scales.
- Cut out your mask and attach the string or elastic to wear it.

Now you're ready to roar like a mighty dragon! Show your family and friends your mask, and maybe even perform a dragon dance.

Write Your Own Trickster Tale: Make Up a Story Starring the Clever Monkey King

The Monkey King is one of the most beloved characters in Chinese mythology. He's mischievous, clever, and always ready for an adventure. Now, it's your turn to come up with your own story featuring this tricky hero!

How to Write Your Trickster Tale:

- Think of a problem. Maybe the Monkey King gets into trouble with another powerful god or needs to rescue a friend.
- Give the Monkey King a clever plan. Remember, he's not the strongest, but he's always the smartest!
- Add some obstacles. Every good story needs a challenge—will the Monkey King's plan work, or will he get caught?
- End with a lesson. Trickster tales often teach something important. Maybe your story is about teamwork, honesty, or thinking before you act.

When you finish, share your story with your family or friends. You might just inspire someone else to become a storyteller too!

Draw Your Favorite Zodiac Animal: Explore the Chinese Zodiac with Art

The Chinese zodiac is made up of twelve animals, each representing a year in a twelve-year cycle. Which animal are you? Here's a chance to explore the zodiac and draw your favorite animal.

Chinese Zodiac Animals:

- Rat
- Ox
- Tiger
- Rabbit
- Dragon
- Snake
- Horse
- Goat
- Monkey
- Rooster
- Dog
- Pig

What to Do:

Pick an animal that speaks to you. Maybe you feel as brave as a tiger or as loyal as a dog.

Use your imagination to give your animal special details. Does your dragon have colorful wings? Is your tiger wearing a crown?

Draw your zodiac animal and give it a name and a personality. You can also write a story about your animal and its adventures in the zodiac.

When you're finished, hang your artwork somewhere special. Your zodiac animal can be a reminder to stay strong, kind, and adventurous—just like the legends!

Map of China: Mark the Places Mentioned in the Legends

Many of the legends in this book take place in beautiful locations across China. Let's make a map to mark the spots where the stories happened!

What You'll Need:

- A printed or hand-drawn map of China
- Markers or stickers
- A list of the legends and the places they are connected to
- Legends and Their Locations:
- The Dragon King: The seas and rivers of southern China

- Chang'e, the Moon Goddess: The sky and the moon
- The Monkey King: The Flower Fruit Mountain and the West
- Yu the Great: The rivers of ancient China
- The Jade Emperor: Heaven and the celestial palace
- The Legend of Mulan: Northern China

Mark each of these places on your map with a star or sticker. You can even decorate your map with small drawings of the characters from the stories!

These activities are just the beginning of your creative journey into Chinese legends. Now that you've designed a dragon mask, written a trickster tale, drawn your favorite zodiac animal, and explored China on a map, what will you do next?

Remember, legends aren't just stories from the past—they are living tales that continue to inspire people today. You can be a part of this tradition by creating your own stories, art, and adventures. So keep dreaming, creating, and sharing your ideas with the world. Who knows? One day, your own legend might inspire others too!

FUN FACTS ABOUT CHINESE CULTURE AND MYTHOLOGY

———— ◆◇◇◉◇◇◆ ————

Welcome to the world of amazing facts about Chinese culture and mythology! Did you know that the legends you've read in this book have been passed down for thousands of years and still inspire art, dance, and movies today? Let's dive into some fun facts about Chinese calligraphy, music, and dance, discover how Chinese myths influence modern stories, and explore famous places where you can experience these legends for yourself.

Amazing Facts About Chinese Calligraphy, Music, and Dance

Chinese culture is full of beauty and tradition. From elegant writing to lively dances, every art form tells a story.

Chinese Calligraphy – The Art of Beautiful Writing

Chinese calligraphy isn't just about writing words; it's a form of art! The brushstrokes represent the writer's emotions and thoughts. There are five main styles of calligraphy, each with its own character. Some are bold and powerful, while others are soft and flowing, just like a river.

Did you know? Calligraphy was so important in ancient China that it was taught alongside reading and math!

Some calligraphy scrolls even tell stories of gods, like the Jade Emperor, or great heroes, such as Mulan. Try practicing calligraphy yourself—you might feel like you're writing your own legend!

Chinese Music – Sounds of the Past

Traditional Chinese music has instruments that create sounds as ancient as the legends. Some popular instruments include the guqin, a seven-string zither, and the erhu, a two-stringed fiddle. Music often tells stories—some songs celebrate brave warriors, while others capture the magic of the moon and stars.

Did you know? Chinese music was believed to connect people with nature and the universe. A performance could reflect the change of seasons or tell the story of the stars.

You might even find songs about Chang'e, the Moon Goddess, or hear sounds inspired by the

Monkey King's adventures in some traditional tunes!

Chinese Dance – Telling Stories Through Movement

Chinese dance is more than just movement—it's storytelling in action. Some dances are energetic and acrobatic, like the Lion Dance performed during the New Year, while others are slow and graceful, like the Fan Dance. These dances are often inspired by legends, animals, and nature.

Fun fact! The Dragon Dance, with performers inside a giant dragon costume, symbolizes power and good luck. It's often performed to scare away bad spirits, just like how the villagers scared away Nian, the New Year monster.

How Chinese Myths Have Influenced Modern Movies and Books

You might not realize it, but some of your favorite books and movies were inspired by ancient Chinese stories!

Movies Inspired by Chinese Myths

The Monkey King has become a well-loved character around the world. His adventures inspired movies like Journey to the West and even influenced the character of Goku in Dragon Ball Z.

The story of Mulan was turned into a famous Disney movie. Her bravery and dedication to family have captured the hearts of people everywhere.

Chinese Symbols in Stories

Dragons, magical creatures, and heroes from Chinese mythology also appear in modern books and games. The idea of a red thread connecting people, as seen in the Legend of the Red Thread of Fate, often shows up in romantic stories. Zodiac animals have also become popular characters in stories for children and adults alike.

Did you know? Even superhero stories often borrow themes from Chinese myths, such as the battle between good and evil or the importance of harmony.

Places to Visit: Famous Temples and Museums to Explore Chinese Legends

If you ever get a chance to visit China, there are some incredible places where you can see history and legends come to life.

The Forbidden City in Beijing

The Forbidden City was once the home of emperors and is filled with statues, art, and stories of the past. You might spot dragons carved into the walls and roofs, guarding the palace just like the Dragon King guards the seas.

The Jade Emperor Pagoda in Shanghai

This beautiful temple is dedicated to the Jade Emperor, the ruler of heaven. Visitors come here to pray for good luck and learn about the Chinese zodiac.

The Temple of the Moon in Beijing

This temple is a perfect place to celebrate the Mid-Autumn Festival and honor Chang'e, the Moon Goddess. It's especially beautiful during the full moon when people gather to enjoy mooncakes and gaze at the night sky.

Museums That Celebrate Chinese Legends

The National Museum of China in Beijing has exhibits about ancient myths, including artifacts related to heroes like Yu the Great and Pangu.

The Shanghai Museum is a treasure trove of Chinese art, including paintings and sculptures that tell legendary stories.

These places are perfect for learning more about the legends that shaped Chinese culture—and maybe even discovering some new ones!

Chinese legends are more than just stories; they are a way to connect with the past and understand the values that shape Chinese culture today. Whether through calligraphy, dance, or a good story, there are many ways to bring these legends to life.

Now it's your turn! Grab a brush and practice writing a message in calligraphy, listen to traditional music, or act out the tale of the Monkey King with your friends. Who knows what kind of legend you'll create? Remember, stories are meant to be shared—so keep exploring, keep creating, and keep passing these amazing tales on to others!

REFERENCES

Below is a list of resources that provided valuable information for the creation of Chinese Legends for Kids. These references include historical texts, cultural studies, folklore collections, and trusted websites dedicated to Chinese history and mythology. They helped ensure the stories and lessons in this book were both accurate and engaging for young readers.

Books and Academic Publications

- Birch, Cyril. Stories from a Ming Collection: The Art of the Chinese Storyteller. New York: Grove Press, 1958.
- Eberhard, Wolfram. Chinese Folktales. University of California Press, 1965.
- Wu Cheng'en. Journey to the West (translated by Arthur Waley). London: Penguin Classics, 1942.
- Idema, Wilt L. Mulan: Five Versions of a Classic Chinese Legend, with Related Texts. Hackett Publishing, 2010.
- Christie, Anthony. Chinese Mythology. Hamlyn, 1975.

Web Resources and Articles

- China Culture. "Chinese Festivals and Their Meanings." www.chinaculture.org.
- Chinese Folk Religion. "The Jade Emperor and the Origins of the Chinese Zodiac."
- China Highlights. "The Legend of Hou Yi and the Ten Suns." www.chinahighlights.com.
- UNESCO World Heritage. "Exploring the Myths Behind the Forbidden City."
- Museums and Cultural Institutions
- The National Museum of China, Beijing. Exhibits on Chinese mythology and folklore.
- Shanghai Museum, Shanghai. Collections of ancient Chinese art reflecting legendary stories.
- Smithsonian Institution, Washington, D.C. Online exhibits featuring traditional Chinese festivals and artifacts.

Documentaries and Media

- Legends of China, documentary series by CCTV.
- The Myth and the Zodiac, educational program by the History Channel.

Traditional Chinese Texts and Translations

- Classic of Mountains and Seas (Shanhaijing), translated by Anne Birrell.
- Records of the Grand Historian by Sima Qian, focusing on legendary rulers.

These references ensured that the book is both entertaining and educational, providing authentic insights into the rich world of Chinese legends. We hope they inspire readers to continue exploring the magic and wisdom of Chinese mythology for years to come.

FREE BONUS FROM HBA:
EBOOK BUNDLE

Greetings!

First, thank you for reading our books.

Now, we invite you to join our VIP list. As a welcome gift we offer the History & Mythology eBook Bundle below for free. Plus, you can be the first to receive new books and exclusives! Remember it's 100% free to join.

Simply click the link below to join.

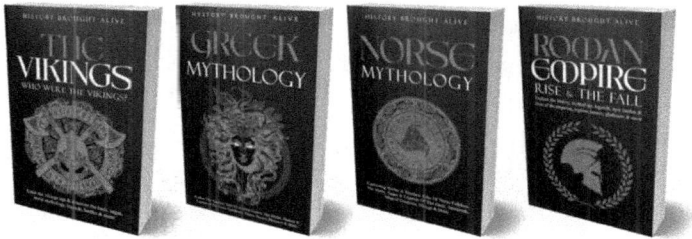

135

Check out the other books in this series

- African Legends For Kids: Kings, Queens, Heroes, Spirits, Myths, Tales & More From Africa
- Aztec Legends For Kids: Gods, Warriors, Myths, Wonders & More From Ancient Mexico
- Celtic Legends For Kids: Heroes, Fairies, Warriors, Myths, Magic & More From The Ancient Celts
- Chinese Legends For Kids: Emperors, Dragons, Gods, Heroes, Myths & More From Ancient China
- English Legends For Kids: Knights, Castles, Kings, Queens, Myths & More From Old England
- Incan Legends For Kids: Emperors, Warriors, Myths, Treasures & More From Ancient Peru
- Indian Legends For Kids: Gods, Goddesses, Warriors, Sages, Myths, Epics & More From Ancient India
- Irish Legends For Kids: Heroes, Druids, Myths, Magic & More From Ancient Ireland
- Japanese Legends For Kids: Samurai, Spirits, Emperors, Myths, Magic & More From Japan

- Mesopotamian Legends For Kids: Kings, Queens, Gods, Myths, Wonders & More From The Cradle Of Civilization
- Native American Legends For Kids: Spirits, Chiefs, Warriors, Myths, Sacred Tales & More
- Persian Legends For Kids: Heroes, Kings, Myths, Epics & More From Ancient Persia
- Russian Legends For Kids: Czars, Fairies, Warriors, Folktales, Myths & More From Russia
- Scottish Legends For Kids: Warriors, Fairies, Kings, Queens, Myths, Legends & More From Scotland
- Thai Legends For Kids: Kings, Queens, Demons, Heroes, Myths, Sacred Tales & More From Thailand
- Viking & Norse Legends For Kids: Gods, Warriors, Myths, Heroes & More From The From The Ancient Norse World
- Welsh Legends For Kids: Dragons, Heroes, Prophecies, Myths, Magic & More From Ancient Wales

and follow us on www.historybroughtalive.com
and
https://www.youtube.com/@historybroughtalive

www.ingramcontent.com/pod-product-compliance
Lightning Source LLC
Chambersburg PA
CBHW051857090426
42811CB00003B/371